QUESTIONS
in STANDARD GRADE
BIOLOGY

Morag Laughlan

Text copyright © 1997 Morag Laughlan
Design and layout copyright © 1997 Leckie & Leckie Ltd

Published by
Leckie & Leckie
8 Whitehill Terrace
St Andrews KY16 8RN
tel: 01334 475656
fax: 01334 477392
email: hq@leckieandleckie.co.uk
web: www.leckieandleckie.co.uk

Edited by Andrew Morton

Special thanks to
Nolan Cocker, Alison Irving, Susanna Kirk,
Bruce Ryan and Hamish Sanderson

ISBN 1-898890-70-6

A CIP Catalogue record for this book is available from the British Library.

Printed in Scotland by Scotprint.

® Leckie & Leckie is a registered trademark.

Leckie & Leckie Ltd is a division of Granada Learning Limited, part of Granada plc.

with answer section

Leckie & Leckie

Contents

Introduction

1. What this book covers

Your Standard Grade Biology course has two main areas of study:
- Knowledge and Understanding, and
- Problem Solving.

This book contains questions and answers on both of these areas.

It is impossible to include in this book questions on everything in your course but you will find that the main topics have questions about them.

To help you in your revision, the questions and answers for General level are printed on a normal, white background (like this).

The extra Credit level questions and answers are printed on a shaded background (like this). Your teacher will tell you whether you need to try the Credit level questions.

2. Leckie & Leckie's *Standard Grade Biology Revision Notes*

We recommend that you obtain a copy of Leckie & Leckie's other Standard Grade Biology book, *Standard Grade Biology Revision Notes*, from your school or bookshop.

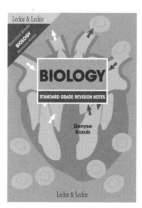

At the foot of every page of questions you will find a page reference to Leckie & Leckie's *Standard Grade Biology Revision Notes*. As you work through the questions, look up these pages to help you with your revision.

3. Using the questions

You can use these questions:
- as homework exercises to help you as you study each topic in your Standard Grade course
- as class exercises during your course
- as part of your final revision when you are getting close to your Standard Grade examination.

4. Using the answers

Specimen answers are provided for each of the questions. These can be found at the back of this book. Try to resist the temptation to look at them.

Although specimen answers to the questions are given in this book, it is only your teacher who can tell you if **your** answer is good enough.

1. The Biosphere

Investigating an Ecosystem

1. In the grass bank represented in the diagram below, biologists discovered a species of poppy and wanted to estimate the abundance of this species in the whole bank. To do this they used a quadrat of area 1 m² as shown in the diagram.

   x = one poppy plant

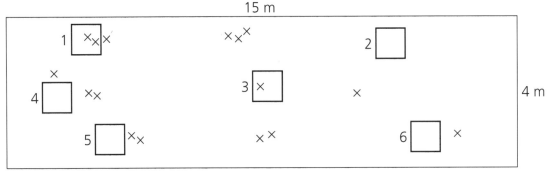

   (a) Copy and complete the table below to show the information collected about the abundance of poppies in the grass bank.

Quadrat	1	2	3	4	5	6
Number of poppies found in quadrat						

   (b) Calculate the:
      (i) average abundance per quadrat (1 m²)
      (ii) area of the grass bank
      (iii) estimated abundance of poppies in the grass bank.

   (c) (i) What is the actual number of poppies in the grass bank?
      (ii) Explain why the actual number is different from the estimated number of poppies.
      (iii) Describe a means of improving the sampling technique to minimise this difference.

2. (a) Identify two abiotic factors which may affect the distribution of poppies in the grass bank.

   (b) (i) Describe a technique which could be used to measure a named abiotic factor.

      (ii) Identify a possible source of error when using this technique and explain how it might be minimised.

      (iii) Explain how this abiotic factor may influence the distribution of poppies in the grass bank.

How it works

3. (a) Match up each of the following terms with its correct meaning by writing each term with its correct meaning beside it.

Term	Meaning
Ecosystem	– all the organisms in an area
Community	– the place where an organism lives
Habitat	– all the organisms of one kind
Population	– all the organisms and their non-living surroundings

(b) Copy and complete the following, using two of the terms above:

Ecosystem = _____ + _____

4.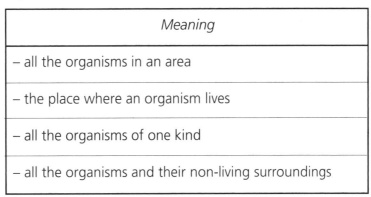

(a) What do the arrows in a food chain or web indicate?

(b) Where does the energy in a food chain come from?

(c) From the food web above, name:
(i) a producer   (ii) a consumer.

(d) Describe and explain the effect of removing all the grass on the population of:
• rabbits   • small birds   • foxes

(e) State two ways in which energy can be lost from this food web.

5.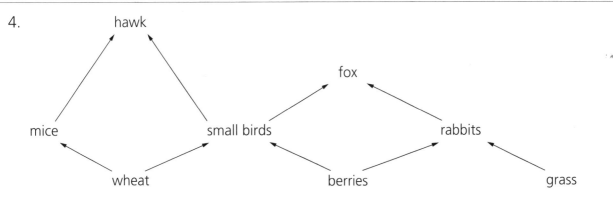

Copy and complete the following sentence, choosing the correct word from each box to complete the sentence:

A pyramid of biomass shows the total number / mass of a population / community at each stage of a food web / chain.

6. (a) 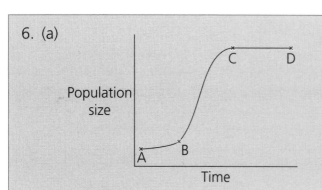 The graph shows population growth after an organism is released into a new area.

Use the terms 'birth rate' and 'death rate' to describe and explain the change in population size from positions:
- B to C
- C to D

(b)

A population explosion	B disease	C competition	D food
E water	F space	G light	H predators

Select the letter(s) of the boxes which best match each of the descriptions below:
(i) two or more organisms requiring the same resources which are in short supply
(ii) the birth rate of a population is much greater than the death rate
(iii) three resources for which plants compete.

7. (a) Phrases A to F below describe stages in the nitrogen cycle. Copy the diagram below and match each phrase to the correct position in the cycle by writing its letter in the correct box in the diagram.

A animal protein   D dead organisms and waste
B nitrates in soil   E nitrite bacteria
C lightning   F nitrate bacteria

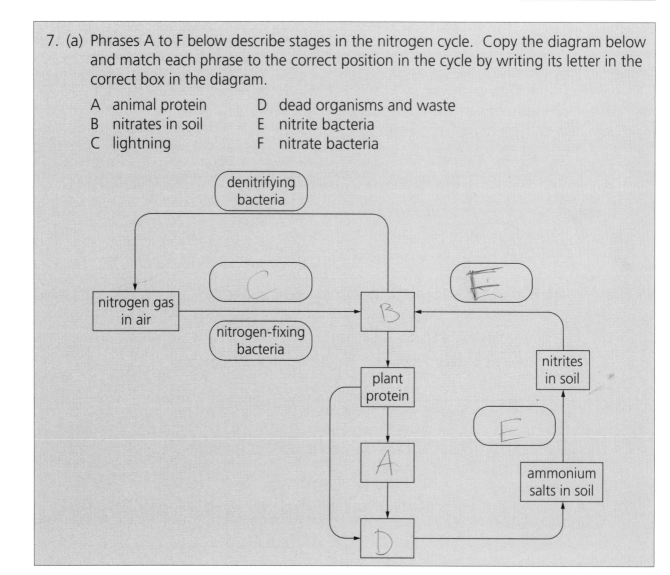

7. (b) Copy the table below and then tick either the true or the false box to indicate whether the statement is true or false. If the statement is false, write the correct word(s) in the correction column to replace the underlined word(s) in the statement.

Statement	True	False	Correction
Bacteria and fungi which release nutrients from dead organisms are called <u>producers</u>.			
All living organisms need nitrogen to make <u>protein</u>.			
Nitrogen-fixing bacteria are found in the roots of <u>all plants</u>.			
Nitrogen fixing means absorbing <u>nitrate</u> into the soil and converting it into a form which plants can use.			

Control and Management

8. A stretch of river was examined for signs of sewage pollution. The diagram below shows the sites where samples were taken and examined for indicator species. The oxygen concentration of the water was measured using methylene blue which changes from blue, at high oxygen concentration, to clear, at low oxygen concentration.

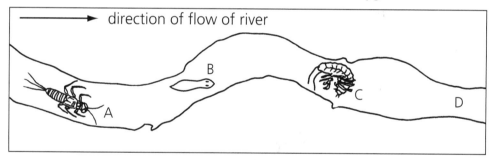

direction of flow of river

(a) What is meant by an indicator organism?

(b) Use the following key to identify the organisms found at each sample site.

1. legs present ...	go to 2	
legs absent ...	go to 3	
2. curved body ...	shrimp	
straight body ...	stonefly nymph	
3. shell present ...	snail	
shell absent ...	flatworm	

Sample site	Indicator Organism
A	
B	
C	

8. (c)

Sample Site	Colour of methylene blue solution
A	dark blue
B	clear
C	light blue
D	dark blue

(i) Between which two sample sites was organic waste released into the river?

(ii) Give a reason for your answer.

(d) Explain the relationships between the following factors:
- levels of sewage pollution
- number of micro-organisms
- oxygen content of water
- variety of species present.

9. Two neighbouring farmers, each with eight equally sized fields, planted their crops in spring. Farmer Brown planted all eight of his fields with wheat. Farmer Jones planted only two of her fields with wheat; she planted two fields with potatoes, two fields with beans and rented her two remaining fields to a local stable for grazing horses. When the crops were harvested and the stables had paid for their use of the grazing land, it was calculated that Farmer Brown had made 18% more profit from his land than Farmer Jones had made from her land.

(a) If both farmers make the same use of their land for the next five years, what problem will Farmer Brown encounter? Give reasons for your answer.

(b) (i) Farmer Jones planted different crops in different fields each year. What is the name of this form of land management?
(ii) What function does the bean crop have in this form of land management?

(c) (i) Give an example of poor management of resources in an ocean environment.
(ii) Suggest a possible method of improving the management of these resources.

10. (a) Copy and complete the table below to show causes and effects of pollution.

Source of pollution	Part of the environment affected	Example of pollutant	Effect of pollutant	Method of control
industry	air			Clean Air Act
		rubbish	eyesore	recycle waste
	fresh water	fertiliser	algal bloom	reduce use of phosphates

(b) Name one energy source which causes pollution. Explain the adverse effects of using this energy source.

Introducing Plants

11. Copy the table below, rearranging the examples to match up with the correct important use of plants.

Important use of plants	Example
ornamental plants	– Both parents are carefully selected when producing new varieties of rose.
raw materials	– Oak trees support a greater number and variety of species than larch.
food source in a food web	– Car tyres are made from rubber.
habitat	– Potato plants convert carbon dioxide and water into starch.
plant breeding	– Oxygen is released during photosynthesis.
gas balance	– Some plants are evergreen, others change colour in autumn.

12. Copy and complete the diagram below to show some specialised uses of plants. For each use of plants, add another example.

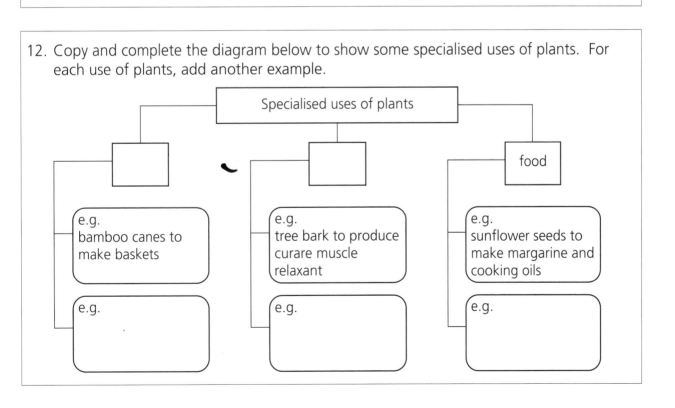

Specialised uses of plants

food

e.g. bamboo canes to make baskets

e.g. tree bark to produce curare muscle relaxant

e.g. sunflower seeds to make margarine and cooking oils

e.g.

e.g.

e.g.

13.

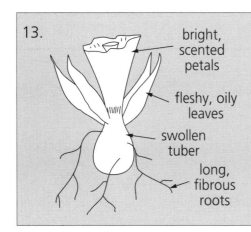

bright, scented petals

fleshy, oily leaves

swollen tuber

long, fibrous roots

The plant shown has a swollen tuber which is used as a food source by some animals in the South American rainforest where it grows.

(a) Describe a potential use of this plant to humans.

(b) Deforestation is resulting in large areas of rainforest being destroyed. Explain one consequence to humans if this plant is wiped out before it has been carefully studied.

Growing Plants

14. Use the terms from the table below to answer questions (a) and (b).

seed-coat	pollination	fruit	clone	food store	tuber	grafting	embryo

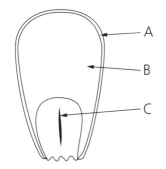

A

B

C

(a) Choose the correct terms from the table to label the diagram of a sunflower seed.

(b) Choose the correct term from the table to match each of the descriptions below.
  (i) transfer of pollen from the anther to the stigma
  (ii) formed from the ovary after fertilisation
  (iii) a method of artificial propagation
  (iv) genetically identical offspring
  (v) plant organ for asexual reproduction

15.

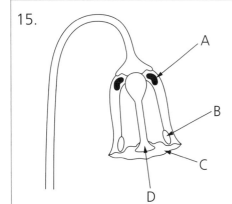

A

B

C

D

Use the information in the diagram of a flowering plant to answer the questions.

(a) Identify the parts of the flowering plant labelled on the diagram.

(b) (i) What method of pollination is used by this plant?
  (ii) Give two reasons for your answer.

(c) When this plant reproduces, it goes through all the following stages. Write out these stages in the correct order, starting with pollination.
  · pollination
  · seed dispersal
  · fertilisation
  · pollen tube growth
  · germination
  · seed and fruit formation

16. Seventy-five oat seedlings were planted in each of three identical seed trays in order to find out how temperature affects seed germination in oats.

Tray 1

4°C in a fridge
100 ml water
10 seeds germinated

Tray 2

20°C in a greenhouse
100 ml water
70 seeds germinated

Tray 3

60°C in an oven
100 ml water
12 seeds germinated

(a) Calculate the percentage germination at each temperature.

(b) Which temperature in the experiment was closest to the optimum temperature for germination of oat seeds?

(c) Identify two variables which were kept constant throughout the experiment.

(d) State one way in which the validity of the experiment could have been improved (to provide a fair comparison).

(e) State one way in which the reliability of the results could be improved.

(f) State three factors which are necessary for germination.

17. (a) Examine the diagrams below. For each fruit, name and describe the method of seed dispersal and give an example of another plant which uses the same dispersal method.

fruit

ash seed

fruit

tomato seed

(b) State two advantages of dispersing seeds away from the parent plant.

18. Decide whether each statement below is true or false. If the statement is false, write the correct word to replace the underlined word(s) in order to make the statement true.

(a) Strawberry plants reproduce <u>sexually</u> by producing runners.

(b) Plants produced by sexual reproduction will have <u>the same</u> characteristics as the parent plants.

(c) <u>Asexual reproduction</u> avoids the vulnerable stages of germination and early growth.

(d) Sexual reproduction is <u>quicker</u> than asexual reproduction.

(e) Plants produced asexually from a single parent make up a <u>clone</u>.

Making Food

19.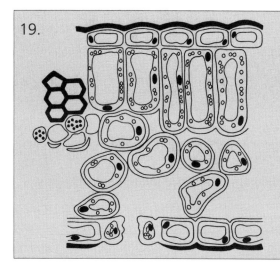

    (a) Copy the diagram which shows the internal structure of a leaf. Add the following labels to your diagram:
    - guard cell
    - air space
    - stoma
    - palisade mesophyll
    - xylem
    - spongy mesophyll
    - phloem
    - epidermis.

    (b) On your diagram, shade in all parts of the leaf where photosynthesis takes place.

    (c) State two features of a leaf which allow it to absorb maximum light for photosynthesis.

20. (a) Copy and complete the word equation for photosynthesis.

Raw materials	Essential requirements	Products
_____ + water	light energy ⟶ chlorophyll	_____ + _____

(b) Describe how each of the raw materials is transported to the photosynthesising cells.

(c) Describe what happens to each of the products of photosynthesis.

21.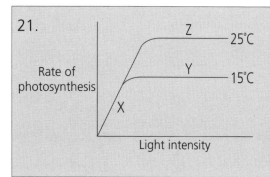

Rate of photosynthesis

Light intensity

Z — 25°C
Y — 15°C
X

The graph shows the rates of photosynthesis in pondweed under different light intensities and temperatures.

(a) Identify the factor which is limiting the rate of photosynthesis at point X and point Y on the graph.

(b) Name another factor which may be responsible for limiting the rate of photosynthesis at point Z.

22.

shoot

root

The diagrams show cross-sections through the shoot and root of a young sunflower plant.

(a) Copy the diagrams and label the xylem and the phloem.

(b) (i) State the two main functions of the xylem.
    (ii) Describe how the structure of the xylem is related to its function.

(c) (i) State the function of the phloem.
    (ii) Describe how the structure of the phloem is related to its function.

See pages 14 and 15 of Leckie & Leckie's *Standard Grade Biology Revision Notes*

3. Animal Survival

The Need for Food

23. Copy and complete the table below to show the chemical composition and biological importance of different food groups to animal survival.

Food group	Sub-units	Chemical elements	Function
	sugar molecules	carbon, hydrogen and oxygen	
fats and oils			energy store, insulation
proteins			

24. Copy and complete the following by choosing the correct word from each box:

Digestion is the breakdown / build up of large soluble / insoluble food particles into small soluble / insoluble particles which can be absorbed through the stomach / small intestine wall into the bloodstream. Digestion involves the chemical / physical breakdown of food by the teeth and the chemical / physical breakdown of food by enzymes. Carbohydrates, fats and proteins are digested by the same / different enzymes.

25.

Jaw A 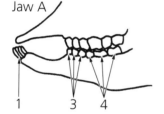   Jaw B 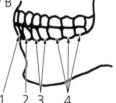   Jaw C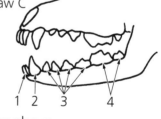

(a) Identify the types of teeth labelled 1 to 4 in the diagrams above.

(b) Copy and complete the table below to provide information about each of the jaws.

Jaw	Diet	Group	Example
A	tough vegetation		sheep
B	mixed		
C	meat	carnivore	

26. (a) Name the parts of the digestive system labelled A to K in the diagram.

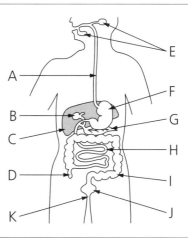

(b) Copy and complete the table below by ticking the true or false box beside each statement. If the statement is false, write the correct word in the correction box to replace the underlined word in the statement.

Statement	True	False	Correction
<u>Amylase</u> produced in the stomach digests protein.			
The <u>liver</u> produces amylase, protease and lipase enzymes.			
The gall bladder stores bile which is necessary for <u>fat</u> digestion.			
Trypsin is a <u>protease</u> which breaks down protein into amino acids.			
The substrate for salivary amylase is <u>maltose</u>.			

27.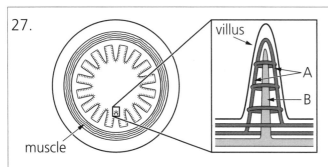

The diagram shows a cross-section through the small intestine of a mammal.

(a) State three ways in which the structure of the small intestine is related to its function of absorbing food.

(b) (i) Explain the function of the muscle in the gut wall.
(ii) What name is given to this process?

(c) (i) Name structures A and B in the diagram of a section through a villus in the small intestine.
(ii) State the function of A and B in the transport of digested food away from the gut.

28. Describe the role of the large intestine using all the words below.

undigested food	large intestine	elimination	anus	absorption	rectum	faeces

Reproduction in Animals

29. (a) Draw and label diagrams of a sperm cell and an egg cell. Your diagrams should include the following labels: cytoplasm, head, tail and nucleus.

(b) Describe the process of fertilisation.

30.

Human male reproductive system

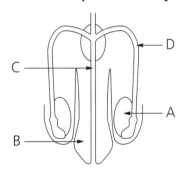

Human female reproductive system

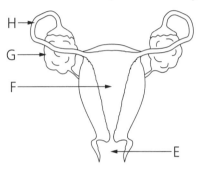

(a) Name the parts labelled A to H on the diagrams.

(b) Identify the following parts by their letter on the diagrams:
  (i) site of sperm production
  (ii) site of egg production
  (iii) where fertilisation takes place
  (iv) where fertilised egg implants and develops
  (v) where sperm are deposited.

31. Study this diagram of an embryo in a uterus.

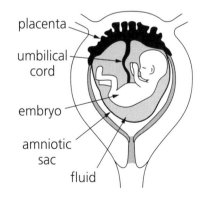

placenta
umbilical cord
embryo
amniotic sac
fluid

(a) Describe the function of the placenta.

(b) Name two waste products which pass from embryo to mother.

(c) Name two substances which pass from mother to embryo.

(d) Name two harmful substances which can pass from the mother's blood to the baby.

(e) Describe the function of the fluid-filled amniotic sac.

32. Construct a table to compare external fertilisation in trout with internal fertilisation in humans.

Your table should include the following information:
- where sperm are deposited
- where eggs are released
- where fertilisation occurs
- food source
- protection of eggs
- number of eggs produced
- survival chances of young
- parental care of young.

Water and Waste

33. Copy and complete the diagram to show how water balance is maintained in a mammal.

Water Gain — Water Balance — Water Loss

34.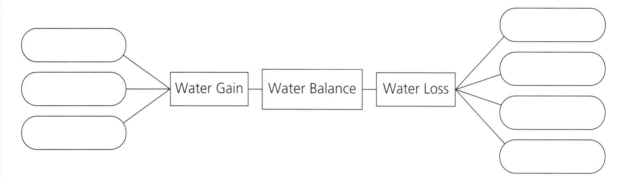

Copy this diagram of an excretory system and then label your diagram using the words in this box.

right kidney	ureter	left kidney
renal artery	renal vein	bladder

35. Choose the correct answer:

(a) The main functions of the kidney are:
   A to break down waste products in the blood and absorb glucose
   B to control water balance and break down urea
   C to filter urea from the blood and control water balance.

(b) The main source of urea in the body is from the breakdown of:
   A amino acids
   B carbohydrates
   C fatty acids.

36. (a) Describe two possible treatments for total kidney failure.

(b) State one advantage of each type of treatment.

37.

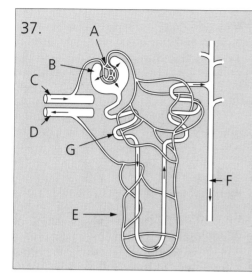

Use the letters in this diagram of a nephron to identify the structures and functions listed below (each letter may be used more than once):
- Bowman's capsule
- glomerulus
- collecting duct
- transports blood to the glomerulus
- site of glucose reabsorption
- transports urine to the ureter

38. Copy and complete the diagram to show the role of ADH (antidiuretic hormone) in the regulation of water balance.

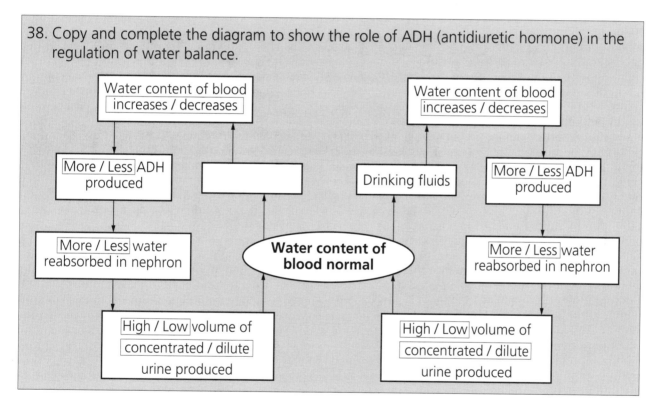

Responding to the Environment

39. An experiment was set up to investigate how earthworms reacted to a choice of environmental conditions in a T-maze.

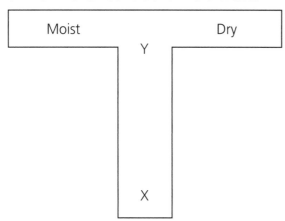

An earthworm was placed at point X in the T-maze. When the worm reached point Y, it had to choose between moving towards the moist area or the dry area. The experiment was repeated three times with each of twenty earthworms of the same species.
The results showed that 80% of the worms moved towards the moist part of the maze.

(a) Which environmental factor was altered in the experiment?

(b) How did the earthworms react to this environmental stimulus?

(c) Suggest a reason why earthworms react in this way.

(d) State two features of the experiment which increased the reliability of the results.

40. Copy the table below, rearranging the descriptions to match up with the correct responses to the environment.

Response to the environment	Description
rhythmical behaviour	– changes in day length resulting in swallows migrating south
trigger stimulus	– the internal mechanism which tells hedgehogs when to hibernate
biological clock	– changes in the way an organism acts as a result of regular environmental changes

41. Name an animal which migrates and describe the advantages of this type of behaviour to the animal concerned.

4. Investigating Cells

Investigating Living Cells

42. Copy and complete the following sentences:
    The basic unit of life is the _____. Most cells are too small to be seen using just eyes and so must be observed using a _____. It is easier to see cell structures if the cells have been _____.

43. Examine the cells shown in the diagrams below.

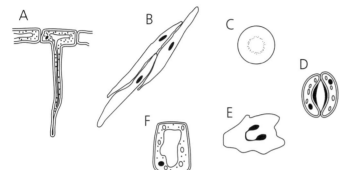

(a) Sort the cells into a group of animal cells and a group of plant cells.

(b) State three features common to both animal and plant cells.

(c) Name three structures which are found only in plant cells.

Investigating Diffusion

44. Copy and complete the following sentences:
    Diffusion is the movement of a substance from where it is in a _____ concentration to where it is in a _____ concentration along a concentration _____. Diffusion continues until the substance is _____ spread out.

45. The amoeba is a single-celled organism which uses diffusion to gain raw materials and get rid of waste.

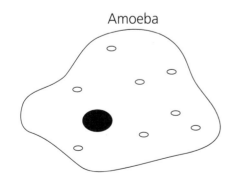

Amoeba

(a) Name two substances which the amoeba will gain by diffusion.

(b) Name the structure which controls the movement of substances into and out of cells.

46. Which of the following phrases describe examples of diffusion?

    A Hot air rising upwards from a fire.

    B Scent spreading across a room.

    C Potatoes swelling up when placed in water.

    D Air escaping from a punctured tyre.

    E Plant roots absorbing water from the soil.

---

47. (a) Describe how diffusion is involved in gas exchange and food transport in humans.

    (b) What is the term used to describe the diffusion of water?

48.

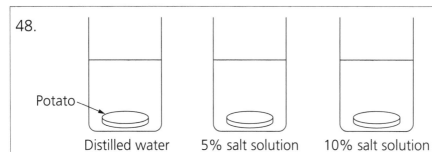

Discs of potato, each weighing 2 grams, were placed in the different solutions shown for 24 hours, then reweighed.

Distilled water   5% salt solution   10% salt solution

Solution	Initial mass (g)	Final mass (g)	Change in mass (g)
distilled water	2·00	3·10	
5% salt solution	2·00	2·00	
10% salt solution	2·00	1·40	

(a) Calculate the change in mass of the potato discs in each solution.

(b) Explain the change in mass in each potato disc.

(c) Describe how the cells of each potato disc would appear when examined under the microscope after 24 hours in solution.

(d) How could the reliability of the results be improved?

(e) Describe what would happen to red blood cells if they were placed in:
    (i) distilled water
    (ii) 10% salt solution.

---

49. Copy and complete the following sentence:
Osmosis is the diffusion of _____ through a _____ _____
membrane along a _____ gradient.

Investigating Cell Division

50. The following diagrams show a cell during different stages of cell division.

X   Y

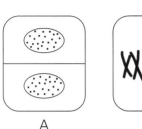   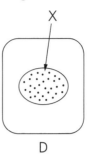 

A   B   C   D   E

(a) Choose the correct sequence from the following to show the order in which the above stages occur during cell division:
   - A, B, C, D, E
   - D, E, C, B, A
   - D, E, B, C, A
   - E, C, B, A, D

(b) Name the structures labelled X and Y in the diagrams.

(c) What name is given to the process shown in the diagrams above?

---

51. Explain why cell division is important in all organisms.

---

52. Name the cell structures which contain all the information required to build a new organism.

---

53. Explain why it is important that the daughter cells produced have the same chromosome complement as the parent cells.

---

54. Describe what is happening in diagrams C and E in question 50.

Investigating Enzymes

55.

enzyme	product	denaturing	specific	synthesis	catalase	substrate	breakdown
carbohydrate		catalyst	optimum	amino acids		amylase	phosphorylase

Choose the correct word from the box above to match each of these descriptions:

(a) A substance which speeds up the rate of a chemical reaction without being used up in the reaction.

(b) A biological catalyst.

(c) The pH or temperature at which an enzyme works best.

(d) A change in enzyme structure which stops the enzyme working.

(e) The molecule on which an enzyme acts.

(f) A type of reaction which joins small molecules together to form larger molecules.

(g) The enzyme which catalyses the build-up of starch in potatoes.

(h) The enzyme which catalyses the breakdown of starch.

(i) The chemicals from which enzymes are made.

(j) The enzyme which breaks down hydrogen peroxide in cells.

56. 1 gram blocks of cooked egg white (protein) were placed in each of the test tubes below. The test tubes were placed in a water bath at 37°C for two hours and then the blocks of egg white were removed and weighed.

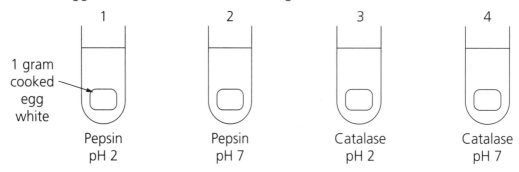

1 gram cooked egg white

1	2	3	4
Pepsin pH 2	Pepsin pH 7	Catalase pH 2	Catalase pH 7

(a) Copy and complete the results table.

Test tube	Mass at start (g)	Mass after 2 hours (g)	Change in mass (g)	% Change in mass
1	1·00	0·05		
2	1·00	0·95		
3	1·00	1·00		
4	1·00	1·00		

56. (b) (i) In which test tube was the egg white digested most rapidly?
    (ii) Explain why.

(c) Explain why the egg white was not digested in test tubes 3 and 4.

(d) Predict the effect on the results for test tube 1 if the experiment had been carried out at:
    (i) 4°C
    (ii) 70°C.
    Explain your answer.

Investigating Aerobic Respiration

57. (a) State three reasons why living cells need energy.

(b) Name the process by which cells use oxygen to release energy from food.

(c) Write out the word equation for this process.

58. Which food groups contain the most energy per gram?

59. The following apparatus was set up to measure respiration rates in peas.

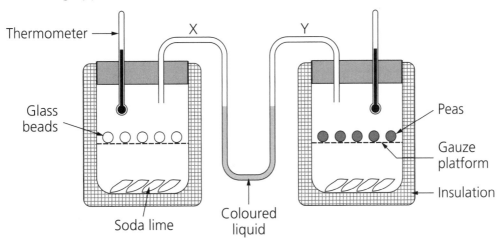

(a) What gas will the peas take in from their surroundings?

(b) What gas will the peas release into their surroundings?

(c) What is the function of the:
    (i) left-hand container
    (ii) soda lime?

(d) (i) Will the coloured liquid move towards X or Y as the peas respire?
    (ii) Explain your answer.

(e) (i) What other change would you expect to observe during the experiment?
    (ii) Explain your answer.

5. The Body in Action

Movement

60. State the three main functions of the skeleton.

61. (a) Copy and complete the table to show the functions of different components of bone.

Component	Function
hard minerals	
	flexibility

(b) Explain why bones need a blood supply.

62. (a) Study the diagrams below and then copy and complete the table to describe joints 1 and 2.

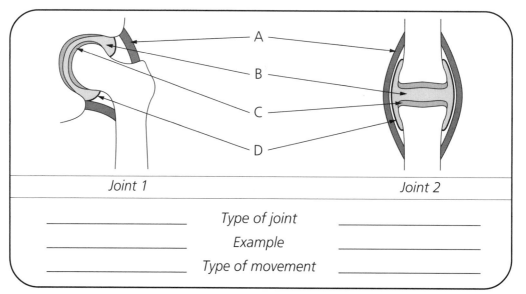

	Joint 1		Joint 2
	_____	Type of joint	_____
	_____	Example	_____
	_____	Type of movement	_____

(b) Use the diagrams of the synovial joints in 62 (a) to copy and complete the table.

Letter	Structure	Function
D		
		holds bones together
	cartilage	
		lubricates joint

63. (a) Look at the four different leg positions below and then copy and complete the table.

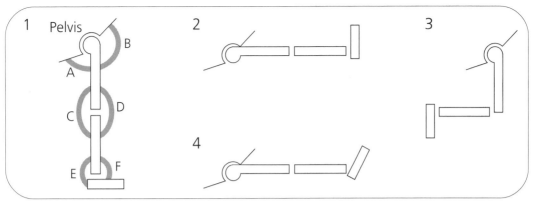

Starting position	Finishing position	Muscles contracted	Muscles relaxed
1	2		
		C	D
	4	E	

(b) Explain how muscles act in pairs to bring about movement of bones.

(c) Copy and complete these sentences by choosing the correct word from each box:

Tendons are elastic / inelastic and attach bones to muscles / bones .

Ligaments attach bones to muscles / bones and are elastic / inelastic .

Tendons / Ligaments are inelastic in order to transmit the force provided by the contracting muscle to the bone.

The Need for Energy

64. (a) Copy and complete the following sentence: Breathing allows _____ gas to enter the body and _____ _____ gas to be removed from the body.

(b) Examine the diagram which shows model lungs, then complete the table to show which structure in the lungs each part of the model represents.

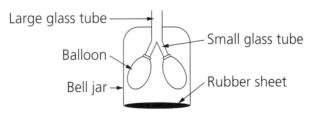

Model Lungs	large glass tube			rubber sheet	bell jar
Real Lungs		bronchus	lung		

65. Describe the self-cleaning mechanism in the lungs.

66. Copy and complete the following sentences, choosing the correct word from each box, to describe inhaling and exhaling air.

During inhalation the ribcage moves down / up and out / in. The diaphragm moves down / up. The volume of the chest cavity decreases / increases causing a decrease / increase in pressure. Air is then forced into the lungs.

During exhalation the diaphragm moves down / up. The ribcage moves out / in and down / up. The pressure / volume of the chest cavity decreases and air is forced out of / into the lungs due to the greater air pressure inside the lungs than outside.

67. Three females with similar weight and build had their energy intake and output measured over a period of three weeks. Their average daily energy intake and output is shown in the table.

Name	Age	Current Occupation	Average energy intake (kJ/day)	Average energy output (kJ/day)
Moira	25	shop assistant	9500	9500
Sarah	25	office clerk	9500	8500
Gwen	25	sportswoman	9500	11 000

(a) Who is most likely to lose weight? Explain your answer.

(b) (i) Calculate how much more energy Sarah takes in than she needs.
(ii) Show this as a percentage of her energy intake.
(iii) How may she store this extra energy?

(c) Describe the relationship between energy intake, energy output, level of activity and weight.

(d) Explain why all three females were monitored for three weeks, rather than just one day.

(e) How could the reliability of the results be improved?

68.

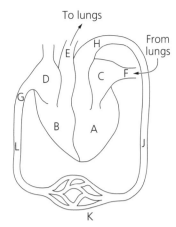

Copy the diagram and

(a) mark the positions of four different heart valves by placing an X on the diagram for each valve

(b) describe the function of heart valves

(c) name the types of blood vessel represented by the letters J, K and L

(d) use the letters on the diagram to copy and complete the boxes below to show the direction of blood flow.

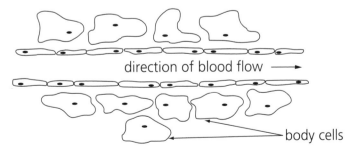

(e) Copy and complete the following sentences, choosing the correct word from each box.

  (i) The right / left ventricle is thicker because it has to pump blood a longer distance.

  (ii) The heart gets its blood supply from the carotid / coronary artery.

  (iii) Arteries / Veins have valves.

  (iv) The pulse rate indicates that blood is flowing through a vein / an artery .

(f) State three features of the capillaries which allow them to exchange materials with body cells efficiently.

69.

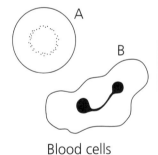

Blood cells

(a) Identify cell type A.

(b) Which substance is transported to the body cells by cell type A?

(c) Use the wordbank below to explain the role of haemoglobin.

lungs	oxygen	diffuses	red blood cells
haemoglobin	oxyhaemoglobin	body cells	

(d) Which component of blood transports soluble food to the cells?

direction of blood flow ⟶

body cells

(e) Name the type of blood vessel shown in the diagram above.

(f) Draw arrows on the diagram to show the direction of movement of oxygen between the blood and body cells.

Co-ordination

70.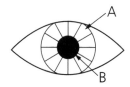

    (a) Identify A and B in the diagram of the eye.

    (b) Describe the changes which would occur to A and B if this person looked into a bright light.

    (c) Copy and complete the following sentences:
       When light enters the eye, the _____ focuses the light onto the _____.
       The light energy is converted to an electrical signal which is carried to the _____ by the _____ nerve.
       Binocular vision involves using _____ eyes. This allows for more accurate judgement of _____.

71.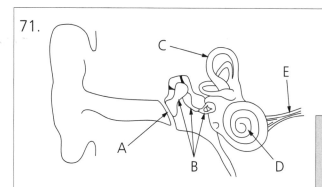

    (a) Name the parts of the ear labelled A to E in the diagram.

    (b) Identify the parts of the ear concerned with hearing.

    (c) Explain how the arrangement of the semicircular canals is related to their function.

    (d) (i) Copy and complete the following sentence:
          The judgement of the _____ of sound is better using two ears rather than one.
       (ii) Explain why.

72. A goalkeeper sees a penalty shot coming towards him. He jumps up and catches the ball, saving the penalty. In order to react in this way the goalkeeper had to send rapid messages through his nervous system.

    Copy and complete the diagram to show the flow of information through the goalkeeper's nervous system.

    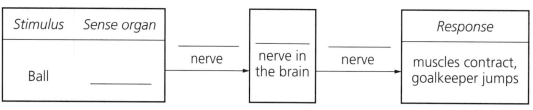

73. (a) What is a reflex action?

    (b) Describe the pathway of nerve impulses involved in the reflex action of blinking.

---

74. State which part of the brain controls each of the following actions:

    (a) a cat balancing on a wall

    (b) an increase in pulse rate after exercise

    (c) answering these questions

    (d) remembering your phone number.

Changing Levels of Performance

75. The graph below shows the results of a study carried out to measure the lactic acid levels in the blood of two individuals before and after exercise.
Use the information in the graph to answer the questions.

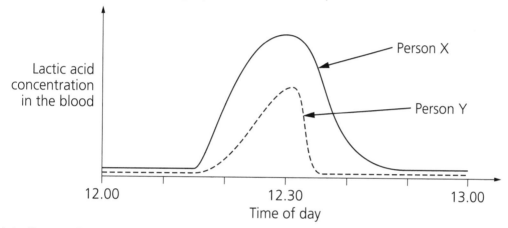

(a) (i) At what time did exercise begin?
      (ii) Give a reason for your answer.

(b) Explain why lactic acid is produced during vigorous exercise.

(c) Write out the equation for anaerobic respiration in muscle tissue.

(d) (i) Of the people studied, which one is likely to be training regularly?
      (ii) Give a reason for your answer.

(e) State two effects not shown in the graph which training would have on the heart.

(f) Define the following terms:
    (i) aerobic respiration
    (ii) anaerobic respiration
    (iii) oxygen debt
    (iv) fatigue
    (v) recovery time.

6. Inheritance

Variation

76. What is a species?

77. Give three examples of variations which occur in the human species.

78. A survey of 100 people was carried out to obtain information about the number of people with each blood group.

Blood group	O	A	B	AB
Number of people	38	15	12	35

(a) Draw a bar graph to show this information.

(b) (i) What type of variation is shown by human blood groups?

(ii) Give a reason for your answer.

79. Five hundred tree seedlings in a nursery were measured three months after planting.

Height (cm)	1–30	31–60	61–90	91–120	121–150	151–180	181–210
Number of trees	10	35	60	100	185	65	45

(a) Draw a bar graph to show the information in the table.

(b) (i) What type of variation is shown by heights of trees?

(ii) Give a reason for your answer.

(c) Give two other examples of this type of variation in plants.

What is Inheritance?

---

80. Where exactly is the genetic information stored which determines the characteristics of an organism?

---

81. State how many sets of chromosomes are found in each of the following cell types:

(a) egg   (b) muscle   (c) pollen   (d) zygote   (e) sperm.

---

82. Describe how the sex chromosomes in humans determine whether offspring are male or female.

---

83. A true-breeding pea plant with red flowers was crossed with a true-breeding pea plant with white flowers.

(a) Copy and complete the diagram to show this monohybrid cross through to the F_2 generation.

Parental phenotype	– True-breeding red flowers	×	_____
Parental genotype	– ___		rr
F_1 genotype	–	All Rr	
F_1 _____	–	All red	

F₁ phenotype   –   Red flowers   ×   Red flowers
F₁ _____   –   ___   Rr

	R	r
R		Rr	Punnett square
r		

F_2 genotypes   –

F_2 phenotype ratio   –   _____ : _____

(b) Circle two individuals in the Punnett square which are true-breeding.

(c) (i) State which flower colour in pea plants is recessive.
    (ii) Give a reason for your answer.

---

84. Use the same layout as shown in question 83 to show the following crosses.

(a) Predict the F_2 phenotype ratio when a true-breeding tomato plant with a hairy stem is crossed with a true-breeding tomato plant with a smooth stem. The offspring all have hairy stems and are self-pollinated.

(b) Predict the F_1 phenotype ratio of a cross between a tall marigold plant (Tt) and a dwarf marigold plant (tt).

(c) Describe the cross you would carry out to determine whether a black mouse had the genotype (Bb) or (BB).

See pages 40, 41, 42 and 43 of Leckie & Leckie's *Standard Grade Biology Revision Notes*

Genetics and Society

85. (a) What is selective breeding?

   (b) Describe an example of selective breeding in plants.

86. A farmer wants to increase his herd of cattle. The key below gives information about the characteristics of a number of different breeds he could use to cross with his existing herd.

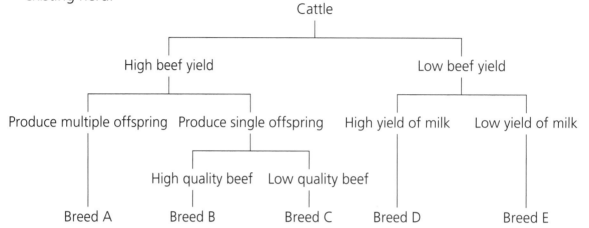

   State which breed the farmer should choose to best increase:

   (a) beef quality

   (b) beef yield

   (c) milk yield.

87. (a) What is a mutation?

   (b) Name a factor which can increase the rate of mutation in an organism.

88. (a) Describe the cause of Down's syndrome in humans.
   (b) How can such mutations be detected before birth?

89. Give an example of a chromosome mutation in plants which is an economic advantage to humans. Give a reason why it is an advantage.

7. Biotechnology

Living Factories

90. 50 ml of bread dough was made up and placed in a measuring cylinder in a warm place for two hours. Its volume was then measured again.

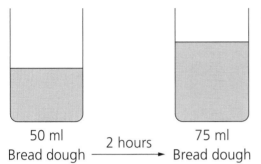

50 ml
Bread dough

2 hours ⟶

75 ml
Bread dough

(a) Name the single-celled organism which is added to bread dough to make it rise.

(b) Write out the word equation for fermentation in bread dough and circle the product of this reaction which makes the bread rise.

(c) Name one other manufacturing process which is dependent on fermentation in yeast.

91. State whether each of the following descriptions is true of aerobic respiration, anaerobic respiration or both, with reference to plants.

(a) requires oxygen   (d) produces carbon dioxide

(b) requires glucose   (e) produces ethanol

(c) requires enzymes   (f) releases energy

92. Brewing involves the following processes:

| Malting of barley | → | fermentation by batch processing | → | collection of ethanol |

(a) Describe the process of malting barley.

(b) Explain why malting is necessary in the brewing industry.

(c) Explain the term 'batch processing'.

(d) What conditions do commercial brewers provide to ensure good growth of yeast?

93. Fresh milk was placed in a sterile test tube containing universal indicator. The colour of the universal indicator was noted at the end of each day for four days to determine the pH of the milk over this time. Table 1 shows the colour of the indicator in the test tube at the end of each day. Table 2 shows the pH indicated by each colour of the universal indicator.

Table 1

Age of milk	1 day	2 days	3 days	4 days
Colour of indicator	green	yellow	orange	red

93. (cont)

Table 2

Colour of indicator	red	orange	yellow	green
pH of solution	1	3	5	7

(a) Draw a line graph to show the effect of the age of milk on its pH.

(b) What group of organisms is responsible for the change in the pH of the milk?

(c) What process do these organisms carry out which results in this change in pH?

(d) Copy and complete the word equation to show this process:

_____ sugar ⟶ _____ acid

(e) Name two manufacturing processes which rely on this reaction.

Problems and Profit with Waste

94. (a) Copy and complete the following sentences:
Untreated sewage dumped into rivers reduces the _____ content of the water. This results in the _____ of animals and the release of foul-smelling _____.

_____ present in sewage can cause diseases such as food poisoning, cholera, _____ and _____.

(b) Rewrite the following stages of sewage treatment in the correct order:
   · Compressed air is pumped into sewage sludge.
   · Sewage is left to settle to the bottom of the tanks.
   · Harmless waste is released into the river.
   · Sewage is screened to remove large objects.
   · Micro-organisms digest the sewage sludge.

(c) Explain why air must be added to ensure the complete breakdown of the sewage.

(d) What do the micro-organisms gain during this process?

95.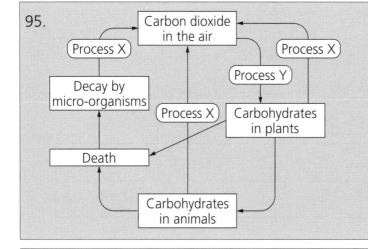

Use the diagram to answer the following questions:

(a) Name Process X and Process Y.

(b) Describe the role of micro-organisms in the process of decay and recycling of nutrients.

(c) Name another nutrient which is recycled in nature by micro-organisms.

96. The following precautions are taken when handling micro-organisms. Explain the reason for each precaution.

(a) Wash hands and wipe bench with disinfectant before starting work.

(b) Sterilise all equipment.

(c) Dispose, at high temperature, of dishes containing micro-organisms.

(d) Wash hands when finished working with micro-organisms.

97. (a) Name a fermentation fuel and describe how it can be produced from waste products.

(b) State two advantages of fermentation fuels over fossil fuels.

(c) (i) Give an example (other than fuel) of waste being upgraded to provide a useful product.
    (ii) Describe the economic importance of this product.

Reprogramming Microbes

98. Four pieces of cloth, each stained with blackcurrant juice, were individually washed for the same length of time in separate solutions as shown below.

Beaker W	Beaker X	Beaker Y	Beaker Z
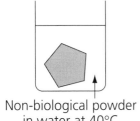	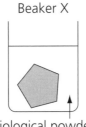	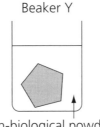	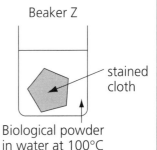
Non-biological powder in water at 40°C	Biological powder in water at 40°C	Non-biological powder in water at 100°C	Biological powder in water at 100°C

stained cloth

Results

Beaker	W	X	Y	Z
Description of each cloth after washing	still stained	completely clean	completely clean	completely clean

(a) (i) What is found in biological powder which accounts for the difference in results between beakers W and X?
   (ii) Explain how this improves the cleaning power of the powder.

(b) Explain why there is no difference in the results obtained in beakers Y and Z.

(c) (i) Which beaker uses the most energy-efficient method of stain removal?
   (ii) Explain your answer.

(d) Describe suitable controls for this experiment.

(e) How could the reliability of the results be improved?

See pages 45, 46, 47 and 48 of Leckie & Leckie's *Standard Grade Biology Revision Notes*   © Leckie & Leckie

99.

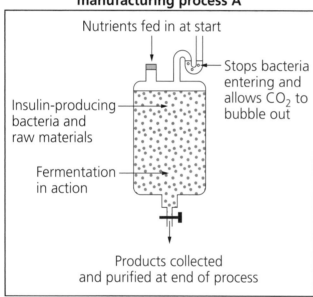

= Bacterial growth

Antibiotic disc

Clear area

A petri dish containing agar with bacteria growing evenly over its surface was prepared. Several antibiotic discs were then placed on the surface of the dish, in contact with the bacteria. The dish was incubated for three days. The appearance of the petri dish after three days is shown in the diagram on the left.

(a) What is an antibiotic?

(b) Which of the antibiotics were effective against these bacteria?

(c) Explain why a range of antibiotics is needed for the treatment of bacterial diseases.

100. The diagrams below show two manufacturing processes which can be used to produce insulin.

Diagram showing manufacturing process A

Nutrients fed in at start

Stops bacteria entering and allows CO_2 to bubble out

Insulin-producing bacteria and raw materials

Fermentation in action

Products collected and purified at end of process

Diagram showing manufacturing process B

Nutrients fed in continuously

Immobilised insulin-producing bacteria

Products collected and purified during process

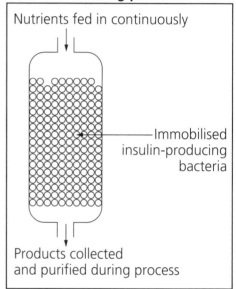

(a) Name manufacturing processes A and B.

(b) What is meant by the immobilisation of bacteria in process B?

(c) Describe two advantages of using immobilisation techniques in manufacturing process B.

(d) Describe how bacteria are changed in order to manufacture human insulin.

(e) Explain the increasing demand for insulin produced by biotechnology.

Answers to Leckie & Leckie's
Questions in Standard Grade Biology

1. The Biosphere

Investigating an Ecosystem

1. (a)

Quadrat	1	2	3	4	5	6
Number of poppies found in quadrat	2	0	1	0	0	0

(b) (i) average abundance per quadrat (1 m²)
= (2 + 0 + 1 + 0 + 0 + 0) ÷ 6 = 3 ÷ 6
= **0·5**
(ii) area of grass bank = 15 m × 4 m
= **60 m²**
(iii) estimated abundance of poppies in grass bank
= average abundance per 1 m² × area of grass bank
= 0·5 × 60 m² = **30 poppies**

(c) (i) 16 (counted from diagram)
(ii) This is only an estimate based on a sample. Estimates are rarely exactly correct.
(iii) Increase sample size by placing more quadrats at random.

2. (a) *Any two of:* · moisture   · temperature
· light intensity · pH.
(b)

	Using a light meter to measure light intensity	Using a moisture meter to measure moisture
(i)	place meter at random in sample area, point light sensor to brightest light source, read scale and record light intensity	place moisture probe firmly in the ground, read scale and record moisture level
(ii)	**Source of error:** shadows/changing sunlight **Minimising error:** do not stand over meter, take several readings and calculate average light intensity	**Source of error:** variations over a small area **Minimising error:** wipe probe dry between readings, take several readings.

Answers for temperature and pH are similar to the answer for moisture, except that the probe should be left in position for 1 to 2 minutes before reading result. Errors arise from not cleaning and drying the probe between readings.

2. (b) (iii) *Any one of the following reasons:*
· moisture – lack of moisture could cause poppies to wilt and die.
· temperature – too high a temperature could cause poppies to dehydrate; too low a temperature could limit the rate of photosynthesis.
· light – low light intensity would limit the rate of photosynthesis.
· pH – extremes of soil pH could inhibit plant growth.

How it works

3. (a)

Term	Meaning
Ecosystem	– all the organisms and their non-living surroundings
Community	– all the organisms in an area
Habitat	– the place where an organism lives
Population	– all the organisms of one kind

(b) Ecosystem = community + habitat

4. (a) the direction of energy flow
(b) the sun
(c) (i) wheat, grass or berries
(ii) hawk, fox, small birds, rabbits or mice

(d)

Organism	Effect on population	Explanation
rabbits	decrease	greater competition (for food)
small birds	decrease	fox eats more birds, competition for food
foxes	decrease	less food

(e) *Any two of:* movement, heat *or* waste

5. A pyramid of biomass shows the total **mass** of a **population** at each stage of a food **chain**.

6. (a)

Stage	Description	Explanation
B to C	rapid increase in population	birth rate much higher than death rate
C to D	no change in population	birth rate equal to death rate

(b) (i) C
(ii) A
(iii) EFG

7. (a)

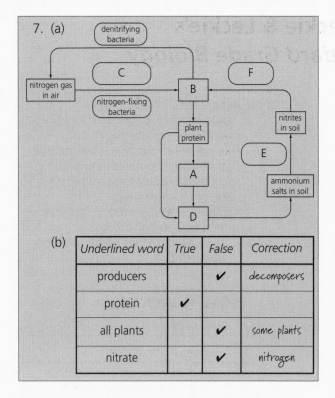

(b)

Underlined word	True	False	Correction
producers		✔	decomposers
protein	✔		
all plants		✔	some plants
nitrate		✔	nitrogen

Control and Management

8. (a) An indicator organism is only present in certain environmental conditions. The presence or absence of the indicator organism allows you to determine the environmental conditions.

(b)

Sample Site	Indicator Organism
A	stonefly nymph
B	flatworm
C	shrimp

(c) (i) between sample sites A and B
(ii) Methylene blue changes from blue to clear indicating low oxygen levels. This shows that bacteria in the sewage are using up the oxygen in the water.

(d) As levels of pollution with organic waste increase, the number of micro-organisms increases. This is because the bacteria in the waste use the waste as a food source to multiply.
The increased number of micro-organisms uses up more oxygen. This results in the oxygen content in the water decreasing. Many species cannot survive with low oxygen concentrations. Therefore the variety of species present decreases.

9. (a) There will be a reduced yield because of reduced minerals in the soil and increased disease.
(b) (i) crop rotation

9. (b) (ii) It contains nitrogen-fixing bacteria in the root nodules. They fix nitrogen into the soil.
(c) (i) e.g. overfishing in the North Sea
(ii) *Either:* increase net mesh size to allow small immature fish to escape.
or: introduce fishing quotas.

10. (a) *There are many possible answers to this question. Here is one:*

Source of pollution	Part of the environment affected	Example of pollutant	Effect of pollutant	Method of control
industry	air	soot	dirty buildings and breathing difficulties	Clean Air Act
domestic	land	rubbish	eyesore	recycle waste
agriculture	fresh water	fertiliser	algal bloom	reduce use of phosphates

(b) **Energy source** — **Adverse effects**
coal, oil and gas (fossil fuels)
· sulphur dioxide and nitrogen oxides cause acid rain
· carbon dioxide causes greenhouse effect and global warming
or
atomic energy — radioactivity causes cancer

2. The World of Plants

Introducing Plants

11.

Important use of plants	Example
ornamental plants	– Some plants are evergreen, others change colour in autumn.
raw materials	– Car tyres are made from rubber.
food source in a food web	– Potato plants convert carbon dioxide and water into starch.
habitat	– Oak trees support a greater number and variety of species than larch.
plant breeding	– Both parents are carefully selected when producing new varieties of rose.
gas balance	– Oxygen is released during photosynthesis.

12.

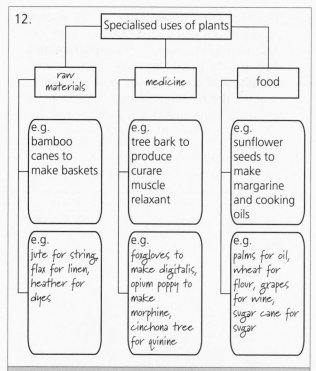

Specialised uses of plants

raw materials
- e.g. bamboo canes to make baskets
- e.g. jute for string, flax for linen, heather for dyes

medicine
- e.g. tree bark to produce curare muscle relaxant
- e.g. foxgloves to make digitalis, opium poppy to make morphine, cinchona tree for quinine

food
- e.g. sunflower seeds to make margarine and cooking oils
- e.g. palms for oil, wheat for flour, grapes for wine, sugar cane for sugar

13. (a) *Any one of the following:*
- extract oil from leaves for cooking
- weave root fibres into rope or cloth
- make perfume from scented petals
- ferment leaves or tuber to make a fuel
- use oil in leaves as a fuel

(b) *Either:* the plant may contain a potential medicine or other potential use to humans which will otherwise never be found

or: this plant may provide a habitat for other plants or animals which may be of potential use to humans. If this habitat is destroyed, all other life which depends upon it is also destroyed.

Growing Plants

14. (a) A = seed-coat
B = food store
C = embryo

(b) (i) pollination
(ii) fruit
(iii) grafting
(iv) clone
(v) tuber

15. (a) A = nectary
B = anther
C = petal
D = stigma

(b) (i) insect pollination
(ii) · produces nectar to attract insects
· sex organs are enclosed within flower
(**Not** scented or brightly coloured petals as this cannot be seen in the diagram.)

(c) 1. pollination
2. pollen tube growth
3. fertilisation
4. seed and fruit formation
5. seed dispersal
6. germination

16. (a) % germination in tray 1
$$= \frac{10 \text{ seeds germinated}}{75 \text{ seeds planted}} \times \frac{100}{1} = \mathbf{13\cdot3\%}$$

% germination in tray 2
$$= \frac{70 \text{ seeds germinated}}{75 \text{ seeds planted}} \times \frac{100}{1} = \mathbf{93\cdot3\%}$$

% germination in tray 3
$$= \frac{12 \text{ seeds germinated}}{75 \text{ seeds planted}} \times \frac{100}{1} = \mathbf{16\%}$$

(b) 20°C
(c) *Any two of:* · number of seeds
· size of tray
· volume of water added.
(d) keep all seeds in the dark
(e) repeat the experiment *or* use more seeds
(f) oxygen, water and a suitable temperature

17. (a)

Seed Type	Ash seed	Tomato seeds
Method of dispersal	wind	animal
Description	shape allows it to 'fly' in the wind	eaten, but not digested, and passed out in animal faeces
Other examples	sycamore, dandelion	cherry, apple and acorn

(b) · reduces competition between parents and offspring for space, light and soil nutrients
· allows the species to colonise new habitats.

18. (a) false, <u>asexually</u>
(b) false, <u>similar</u>
(c) true
(d) false, <u>slower</u>
(e) true

Making Food

19. (a) and (b)

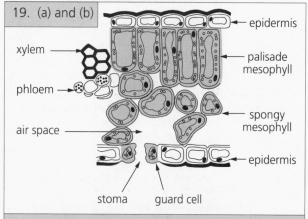

xylem, phloem, air space, epidermis, palisade mesophyll, spongy mesophyll, epidermis, stoma, guard cell

(c) *Any two of:* large surface area, many chloroplasts in upper leaf, palisade cells vertical to allow light to penetrate deep into leaf.

20. (a)

Raw materials	Essential requirements	Products
carbon dioxide + water	light energy → chlorophyll	glucose + oxygen

(b) **carbon dioxide** – enters leaf through stomata then diffuses into the photosynthesising cells
water – enters roots by osmosis, carried in the xylem to the leaf vein and into the cells

(c) **glucose** – used as an energy source in the cell, stored as starch in the cell, transported in the phloem to storage organs/growing parts/developing fruits
oxygen – used by cell for respiration, diffuses out of cell and leaves the leaf through the stomata

21. (a) X = light intensity; Y = temperature
(b) carbon dioxide concentration

22. (a)

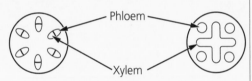

(b) (i) transports water and minerals, provides support for plant
(ii) Hollow, dead columns of cells transport water. Lignin in cell walls provides strength and support.
(c) (i) transports soluble food
(ii) Perforated end walls of sieve tubes allow cytoplasm containing soluble food to flow from one cell to the next.

3. Animal Survival

The Need for Food

23.

Food group	Sub-units	Chemical elements	Function
carbohydrates	sugar molecules	carbon, hydrogen, oxygen	provide energy
fats and oils	fatty acids and glycerol	carbon, hydrogen, oxygen	energy store, insulation
proteins	amino acids	carbon, hydrogen, oxygen, nitrogen	growth and repair

24. Digestion is the **breakdown** of large **insoluble** food particles into small **soluble** particles which can be absorbed through the **small intestine** wall into the bloodstream. Digestion involves the **physical** breakdown of food by the teeth and the **chemical** breakdown of food by enzymes. Carbohydrates, fats and proteins are digested by **different** enzymes.

25. (a) 1 = incisors 3 = premolars
2 = canines 4 = molars

(b)

Jaw	Diet	Group	Example
A	tough vegetation	herbivore	sheep
B	mixed	omnivore	human
C	meat	carnivore	dog

26. (a) A = gullet/oesophagus G = pancreas
B = gall bladder H = small intestine
C = liver I = large intestine
D = appendix J = rectum
E = salivary glands K = anus
F = stomach

(b)

Statement	True	False	Correction
Amylase produced in the stomach digests protein.		✔	pepsin
The liver produces amylase, protease and lipase enzymes.		✔	pancreas
The gall bladder stores bile which is necessary for fat digestion.	✔		
Trypsin is a protease which breaks down protein into amino acids.	✔		
The substrate for salivary amylase is maltose.		✔	starch

27. (a) *Any three of the following:*
- The small intestine is long and folded to increase the surface area for absorption of food.
- Its surface area is increased by the presence of villi.
- It has thin walls which allow food to pass through quickly.
- It has good blood and lymph supplies to carry away rapidly products of digestion.

(b) (i) Muscle behind the food contracts while muscle in front of food relaxes causing food to be pushed through the gut.
(ii) peristalsis

27. (c) (i) A = blood capillary; B = lacteal
    (ii) The blood transports glucose and amino acids away from the gut. The lacteals transport fats away from the gut.

28. Undigested food passes into the large intestine where water absorption takes place. The waste is formed into faeces which are stored in the rectum before elimination from the body through the anus.

Reproduction in Animals

29. (a)

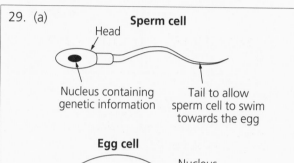

Sperm cell

Head

Nucleus containing genetic information

Tail to allow sperm cell to swim towards the egg

Egg cell

Nucleus

Cytoplasm containing a large food store

(b) Fertilisation is the fusion of the nuclei of a male and a female sex cell.

30. (a) A = testis   E = vagina
       B = penis   F = uterus
       C = urethra   G = ovary
       D = sperm tube   H = oviduct
    (b) (i) A (testis)
        (ii) G (ovary)
        (iii) H (oviduct)
        (iv) F (uterus)
        (v) E (vagina)

31. (a) The placenta is a membranous structure which separates the mother's blood from the embryo's blood. It allows substances to pass between the mother's blood and the embryo's blood.
    (b) carbon dioxide and urea
    (c) oxygen and food
    (d) *Any two of the following:*
        · alcohol
        · nicotine
        · drugs.
    (e) The fluid cushions the embryo from bumps and knocks.

32.

Internal Fertilisation in humans	External Fertilisation in trout
sperm deposited inside vagina	sperm deposited in water
eggs released into oviduct	eggs released into water
fertilisation in oviduct	fertilisation in water
food provided by mother	food from yolk in egg
eggs protected in mother's body	flexible protective egg coating
small number of eggs produced	large number of eggs produced
survival chances of young high	survival chances of young low
parental care of young after birth	no parental care for young

Water and Waste

33.

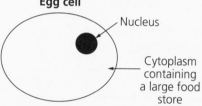

Food

Drinking

Respiration

Water Gain

Water Balance

Water Loss

Urine

Faeces

Sweat

Breathing

34.

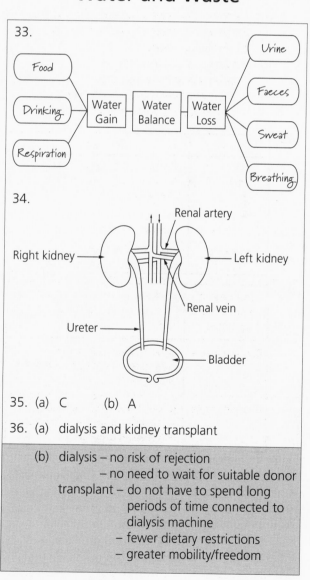

Renal artery

Right kidney

Left kidney

Renal vein

Ureter

Bladder

35. (a) C   (b) A

36. (a) dialysis and kidney transplant
    (b) dialysis – no risk of rejection
                 – no need to wait for suitable donor
        transplant – do not have to spend long periods of time connected to dialysis machine
                 – fewer dietary restrictions
                 – greater mobility/freedom

37. Bowman's capsule – B
    glomerulus – A
    collecting duct – F
    transports blood to the glomerulus – C
    site of glucose reabsorption – G
    transports urine to the ureter – F

38.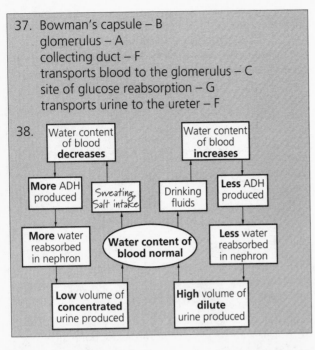

Responding to the Environment

39. (a) moisture
    (b) Earthworms moved towards the moisture.
    (c) Earthworms need a moist surface in order
         to exchange gases.
    (d) *Any two of the following:*
         · twenty worms were used
         · each worm was tested three times
         · all the worms were the same species.

40.

Response	Description
rhythmical behaviour	–changes in the way an organism acts as a result of regular environmental changes
trigger stimulus	–changes in day length resulting in swallows migrating south
biological clock	–the internal mechanism which tells hedgehogs when to hibernate

41.

Example of animal that migrates	Advantages of this type of behaviour to animal
Barnacle geese	breed in Iceland to escape predators, migrate to Scotland in winter for food
Atlantic salmon	breed in Scotland, migrate to Atlantic coast of Greenland for rich feeding grounds

4. Investigating Cells

Investigating Living Cells

42. The basic unit of life is the <u>cell</u>. Most cells are
    too small to be seen using just eyes and so must
    be observed using a <u>microscope</u>. It is easier to see
    cell structures if the cells have been <u>stained</u>.

43. (a) Animal cells: B, C and E
         Plant cells: A, D and F
    (b) nucleus, cell membrane and cytoplasm
    (c) cell wall, chloroplasts and large permanent
         vacuole

Investigating Diffusion

44. Diffusion is the movement of a substance from
    where it is in a <u>high</u> concentration to where it is
    in a <u>low</u> concentration along a concentration
    <u>gradient</u>. Diffusion continues until the substance
    is <u>evenly</u> spread out.

45. (a) *Any two of:*
         · oxygen
         · water
         · dissolved salts.
    (b) cell membrane

46. B, C and E

47. (a) Oxygen diffuses from the air sacs in the
         lungs into the blood and from the blood
         into the cells.
         Carbon dioxide diffuses from the cells into
         the blood and from the blood into the air
         sacs in the lungs.
         Soluble food diffuses from the small
         intestine into the blood, and then from the
         blood into the cells.

    (b) osmosis

48. (a) & (b)

Solution	Change in mass (g)	Explanation
distilled water	+1.10	water enters cells by osmosis
5% salt solution	0.00	water gain equals water loss
10% salt solution	–0.60	water leaves cells by osmosis

    (c) The cell in distilled water would be turgid.
         The cell in 5% salt solution would be
         unchanged.
         The cell in 10% salt solution would be
         plasmolysed.

48. (d) Use more discs of potato in each solution, repeat the experiment and calculate average changes in mass.

   (e) (i) They would burst.
      (ii) They would shrink.

49. Osmosis is the diffusion of _water_ through a _selectively permeable_ membrane along a _concentration_ gradient.

Investigating Cell Division

50. (a) D, E, B, C, A
   (b) X = nucleus; Y = chromosome
   (c) mitosis

51. Cell division is important to increase the number of cells in an organism for growth and repair.

52. chromosomes

53. New cells must have the same chromosome complement as the parent cells so that they have all the information required to build a new organism, produce new cells for growth and replace or repair damaged parts of the organism.

54. C – The chromatids are pulled apart towards opposite ends of the cell.
   E – The chromosomes shorten and thicken and become visible as pairs of chromatids.

Investigating Enzymes

55. (a) catalyst   (f) synthesis
   (b) enzyme   (g) phosphorylase
   (c) optimum   (h) amylase
   (d) denaturing   (i) amino acids
   (e) substrate   (j) catalase

56. (a)

Test tube	Mass at start (g)	Mass after 2 hours (g)	Change in mass (g)	% Change in mass
1	1·00	0·05	–0.95	–95%
2	1·00	0·95	–0.05	–5%
3	1·00	1·00	0.00	0%
4	1·00	1·00	0.00	0%

   (b) (i) test tube 1
      (ii) Pepsin is specific for the substrate protein. Pepsin has an optimum pH of 2.

56. (c) Test tubes 3 and 4 contain the enzyme catalase which does not act on protein. (Catalase is specific to the substrate hydrogen peroxide.)

   (d) (i) At 4°C the reaction would be much slower.
      (ii) At 70°C the reaction would stop.

   Explanation: enzymes work slowly at low temperatures. The rate of an enzyme-catalysed reaction increases as the temperature increases. However, if the temperature gets too high the enzyme is denatured and does not work.

Investigating Aerobic Respiration

57. (a) movement/growth/reproduction/cell division
   (b) aerobic respiration
   (c) glucose + oxygen ⟶ carbon dioxide + water + energy

58. fats and oils

59. (a) oxygen
   (b) carbon dioxide
   (c) (i) It acts as a control.
      (ii) The soda lime absorbs carbon dioxide.
   (d) (i) Y
      (ii) Peas use up oxygen, but the carbon dioxide they release is absorbed by the soda lime. This results in a decrease in the volume of gas on this side of the apparatus and the coloured liquid moves in to take the place of the gas which has been used up.
   (e) (i) increase in temperature in right-hand container
      (ii) When the peas respire, some of the energy is released as heat which increases the temperature of the surroundings. The increase in temperature could be detected on the thermometer.

5. The Body in Action

Movement

60. The three main functions of the skeleton are to:
   · support weight
   · protect vital organs
   · provide a framework for muscle attachment.

61. (a)

Component	Function
hard minerals	strength and hardness
living cells	flexibility

(b) Bones are made up of living cells which require food and oxygen. These are transported to bone cells in the blood.

62. (a)

Joint 1		Joint 2
ball and socket	Type of joint	hinge
hip/shoulder	Example	knee/elbow/finger
all directions/ 3 planes	Type of movement	back and forward/1 plane (**not** '1 direction' as this implies one-way movement only e.g. bend arm only, rather than bend and straighten)

(b)

Letter	Structure	Function
D	synovial membrane	produces synovial fluid
A	ligament	holds bones together
C	cartilage	shock absorber
B	synovial fluid	lubricates joint

63. (a)

Starting position	Finishing position	Muscles contracted	Muscles relaxed
1	2	B	A
1	3	C	D
2	4	E	F

(b) *Either:* when one muscle contracts, the other is relaxed
or: one muscle bends the joint, the other muscle straightens the joint.

(c) Tendons are **inelastic** and attach bones to **muscles**.
Ligaments attach bones to **bones** and are **elastic**.
Tendons are inelastic in order to transmit the force provided by the contracting muscle to the bone.

The Need for Energy

64. (a) Breathing allows oxygen gas to enter the body and carbon dioxide gas to be removed from the body.

(b)

Model Lungs	Real Lungs
large glass tube	trachea
small glass tube	bronchus
balloon	lung
rubber sheet	diaphragm
bell jar	ribcage

65. Dirt and germs are trapped by the sticky mucus. The cilia (small hairs) sweep the dirt and mucus upwards and out of the lungs.

66. During inhalation the ribcage moves **up** and **out**. The diaphragm moves **down**. The volume of the chest cavity **increases** causing a **decrease** in pressure. Air is then forced into the lungs. During exhalation the diaphragm moves **up**. The ribcage moves **in** and **down**. The **volume** of the chest cavity decreases and air is forced **out of** the lungs due to the greater air pressure inside the lungs than outside.

67. (a) Gwen. She uses up more energy than she consumes as she is in an active job.

(b) (i) Sarah: energy intake = 9500 kJ, energy output = 8500 kJ
excess = 9500 – 8500 = **1000 kJ**

(ii) $\dfrac{1000}{9500} \times \dfrac{100}{1} =$ **10.53%**

(iii) She may store the extra energy as fat.

(c) *Either:* If energy intake is higher than energy output due to a low level of activity and a high food intake, then the extra energy is stored as fat, resulting in weight gain.
or: If energy intake is lower than energy output due to a high activity level or low food intake, fat stores are used up, resulting in weight loss.

(d) Monitoring over three weeks reduces the effects of weight variations due to other factors and increases the validity of the experiment.

(e) The reliability could be improved by using more people in the survey (a larger sample size).

68. (a)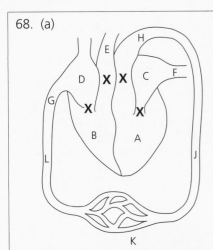

Valves should be marked between atrium and ventricle on both sides of the heart and in the aorta and pulmonary arteries where they leave the heart.

(b) Valves prevent backflow of blood/keep blood flowing in the right direction.

(c) J = Artery, K = Capillary and L = Vein

(d) G–D–B–E–Lungs–F–C–A–H–J–K–L

(e) (i) The **left** ventricle is thicker because it has to pump blood a longer distance.
(ii) The heart gets its blood supply from the **coronary** artery.
(iii) **Veins** have valves.
(iv) The pulse rate indicates that blood is flowing through **an artery**.

(f) · thin walls
· large surface area
· moist surface

69. (a) A is a red blood cell.
(b) The substance is oxygen.

(c) Haemoglobin in the red blood cells combines with oxygen in the lungs to form oxyhaemoglobin. This is transported in the blood to the body cells where the oxyhaemoglobin releases the oxygen. The oxygen then diffuses from the blood into the body cells.

(d) The component is plasma.
(e) capillary
(f)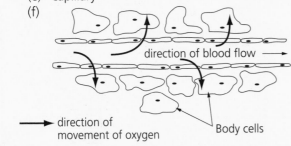

direction of blood flow →

→ direction of movement of oxygen

Body cells

Co-ordination

70. (a) A = iris; B = pupil
(b) A (iris) would contract making B (pupil) smaller

70. (c) When light enters the eye, the lens focuses the light onto the retina. The light energy is converted to an electrical signal which is carried to the brain by the optic nerve. Binocular vision involves using *two* eyes. This allows for more accurate judgement of *distance*.

71. (a) A = eardrum
B = middle ear bones (ossicles)
C = semicircular canals
D = cochlea
E = auditory nerve
(b) A, B, D and E

(c) Each canal is filled with fluid and lies at a different angle. Movements of the head cause the fluid to move. This movement of fluid is detected by nerve endings which send information about head movements to the balance centre in the brain.

(d) (i) The judgement of the *direction* of sound is better using two ears rather than one.
(ii) Each ear detects slightly different sounds. The brain compares the information it receives from each ear to determine the direction of the sound.

72.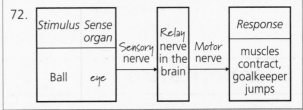

Stimulus	Sense organ				Response
Ball	eye	Sensory nerve	Relay nerve in the brain	Motor nerve	muscles contract, goalkeeper jumps

73. (a) A rapid, automatic response to a stimulus
(b)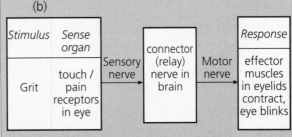

Stimulus	Sense organ				Response
Grit	touch / pain receptors in eye	Sensory nerve	connector (relay) nerve in brain	Motor nerve	effector muscles in eyelids contract, eye blinks

74. (a) cerebellum (c) cerebrum
(b) medulla (d) cerebrum

Changing Levels of Performance

75. (a) (i) 12.15
(ii) Lactic acid concentration increased at this time as a result of anaerobic respiration in the muscle cells.
(b) Lack of oxygen to muscles results in much anaerobic respiration.
(c) glucose ⟶ lactic acid + energy

75. (d) (i) person Y
    (ii) *Any one of the following*:
      · shorter recovery time
      · does not produce as much lactic acid during exercise
      · lactic acid level rises more slowly during exercise.

(e) *Any two of the following*:
  · increased heart volume
  · lower resting heart rate
  · improved coronary circulation
  · increased power.

(f) (i) respiration with oxygen
    glucose $\longrightarrow$ energy + carbon dioxide
      +   + water
    oxygen
  (ii) respiration without oxygen
    glucose $\longrightarrow$ energy + lactic acid
                        (in muscle)
  (iii) the quantity of oxygen which must be breathed in to break down the lactic acid built up as a result of anaerobic respiration
  (iv) muscle tiredness and reduced efficiency as a result of the build-up of lactic acid
  (v) the time taken for pulse rate/breathing rate/lactic acid levels to return to normal after exercise

6. Inheritance

Variation

76. A species is a group of organisms which can interbreed to produce fertile offspring.

77. *Any three reasonable answers: e.g.*
  · height   · hand span   · fingerprints
  · weight   · eye colour   · shoe size.

78. (a)

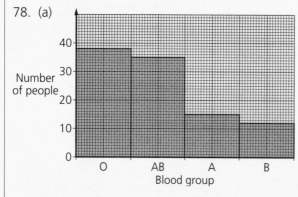

(b) (i) discontinuous variation

  (ii) Individuals show clear-cut differences which can be put into two or more distinct groups.

79. (a)

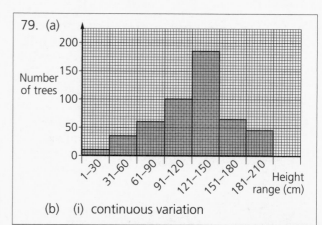

(b) (i) continuous variation

  (ii) Individual trees show a wide range of values which can be measured but cannot be put into distinct groups.

(c) *Any two reasonable answers: e.g.*
  · number of leaves
  · length of roots
  · diameter of stem
  · mass of seeds.

What is Inheritance?

80. The genetic information is found on genes in chromosomes in the nucleus of the cell.

81. (a) 1   (b) 2   (c) 1   (d) 2   (e) 1

82. Males have one X and one Y sex chromosome (XY).
Females have two X chromosomes (XX).
Offspring inherit one sex chromosome from each parent.

male (sperm) \ female (egg)	X	X
X	XX	XX
Y	XY	XY

50% of offspring will be female (XX)
50% of offspring will be male (XY)

83. (a) and (b)

Parental phenotype –	True-breeding red flowers	×	True-breeding white flowers
Parental genotype –	RR		rr
F₁ genotype –		All Rr	
F₁ phenotype –		All red	
F₁ phenotype –	Red flowers	×	Red flowers
F₁ genotype –	Rr		Rr

F₂ genotypes –
×	R	r
R	RR	Rr
r	Rr	rr
Punnett square

F₂ phenotype ratio – 3 red : 1 white

(c) (i) White flower colour is recessive.
  (ii) When one red gene and one white gene are present in the genotype, all the flowers show the red phenotype.

84. (a)

Parental phenotype –	True-breeding hairy stem	×	True-breeding smooth stem
Parental genotype –	HH		hh
F_1 genotype –		All Hh	
F_1 phenotype –		All hairy	

F_1 phenotype –	Hairy stem	×	Hairy stem
F_1 genotype –	Hh		Hh

F_2 genotypes –

X	H	h
H	HH	Hh
h	Hh	hh

Punnett square

F_2 phenotype ratio – 3 hairy stem : 1 smooth stem

(b)

Parental phenotype –	Tall marigold	×	Dwarf marigold
Parental genotype –	Tt		tt

F_1 genotypes –

X	T	t
t	Tt	tt
t	Tt	tt

Punnett square

F_1 phenotype ratio – 1 tall : 1 dwarf

(c) Cross both mice with a recessive mouse (bb). If the black mouse is heterozygous (Bb), only half the offspring will be black. If the black mouse is homozygous (BB), all the offspring will be black.

Genetics and Society

85. (a) the breeding together of individuals in the hope of combining useful characteristics from each parent in the offspring

(b) A disease-resistant variety of wheat can be bred with a high-yield variety to produce a disease-resistant, high-yield variety.

86. (a) Breed B   (b) Breed A   (c) Breed D

87. (a) An abnormal change in the genetic information in the chromosomes of an organism.

(b) *e.g.* α-rays, β-rays, γ-rays, X-rays, UV light, cigarette smoke

88. (a) a chromosome mutation which results in the offspring having an extra chromosome in each cell (47 instead of 46)

(b) Amniocentesis. Fluid is removed from the amniotic sac (which contains cells from the baby). The cells are grown and checked for chromosome defects. The fluid is tested for the presence of chemicals which may indicate chromosome abnormalities.

89. Extra chromosomes in spinach, sugar beet and cereal crops increase the vigour of the plant, increasing yield and, therefore, increasing profit for the farmer.

7. Biotechnology

Living Factories

90. (a) yeast
    (b) glucose → carbon dioxide + alcohol + energy
    (c) brewing *or* wine making

91. (a) aerobic   (d) both
    (b) both   (e) anaerobic
    (c) both   (f) both

92. (a) Barley is germinated to allow enzymes to convert starch in the seed to sugar (maltose).
    (b) Yeast can ferment sugars (e.g. maltose) but cannot ferment starch.
    (c) Raw materials are placed in a large vessel (fermenter) and given the best conditions to promote fermentation. The system is closed and left until fermentation is complete, then the products are collected and purified.
    (d) The yeast is placed in a large, sterile vessel (fermenter) and provided with water, sugar and a supply of minerals. The whole system is closed, kept warm and left until fermentation is complete.

93. (a)

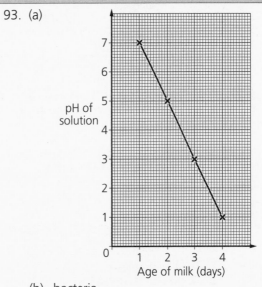

(b) bacteria
(c) fermentation

(d) *lactose* sugar ▭▬ *lactic* acid

(e) cheese production and yoghurt production

Problems and Profit with Waste

94. (a) Untreated sewage dumped into rivers reduces the _oxygen_ content of the water. This results in the _death_ of animals and the release of foul-smelling _gases_. _Micro-organisms_ present in sewage can cause diseases such as food poisoning, cholera, _typhoid_ and _dysentery_.
    (b) • Sewage is screened to remove large objects.
        • Sewage is left to settle to the bottom of the tanks.
        • Compressed air is pumped into sewage sludge.
        • Micro-organisms digest the sewage sludge.
        • Harmless waste is released into the river.
    (c) Oxygen is needed to allow the microbes to respire aerobically.
    (d) Micro-organisms use the sewage as a source of raw materials and energy.

95. (a) X = respiration; Y = photosynthesis
    (b) The micro-organisms release the nutrients locked inside the dead organisms when they break down the dead tissue to provide themselves with a food source.
    (c) e.g. nitrogen, phosphorus

96. (a) to prevent contamination of equipment with micro-organisms from skin or bench
    (b) to ensure that only the micro-organisms being studied are growing
    (c) to ensure that all micro-organisms are killed after experiment is completed
    (d) to prevent you being contaminated with the micro-organisms you have been working with

97. (a) _Either:_ methane gas – released when micro-organisms are grown on fresh manure
        _or:_ alcohol – produced when yeast is grown on sugar.
    (b) Fermentation fuels will not run out and do not pollute the air.
    (c) (i) Fruit pulp can be used to grow protein-rich micro-organisms.
        (ii) The protein-rich fungus can be used as animal feed. The energy in the fruit pulp is no longer wasted.

Reprogramming Microbes

98. (a) (i) enzymes
        (ii) Enzymes digest protein stains at low temperatures.
    (b) At high temperatures the enzymes are denatured. When this happens, the biological detergent relies on other cleaning agents in the same way as non-biological detergents.
    (c) (i) Beaker X
        (ii) removes stains at lower temperatures reducing the cost of heating the water
    (d) • beaker containing only stained cloth and water at 40°C
        • beaker containing only stained cloth and water at 100°C
    (e) repeat the experiment/use several pieces of stained cloth in each beaker

99. (a) a chemical which prevents the growth/ reproduction of bacteria.
    (b) C and D
    (c) Different antibiotics are effective against different bacteria/some bacteria are resistant to some antibiotics.

100. (a) A = batch processing; B = continuous flow processing
     (b) The bacteria are fixed onto glass beads or jelly.
     (c) The same bacteria can be used over and over again.
         There is no need to separate the bacteria from the product.
     (d) Human cells are grown and the chromosome containing the insulin gene is isolated.
         The insulin gene is 'cut' out of the chromosome using enzymes.
         Bacteria are grown and bacterial plasmids are removed.
         The insulin gene is inserted into the bacterial plasmids.
         The plasmids are put back into the bacteria.
         The bacteria reproduce rapidly.
         Each bacterium produces insulin which is collected and purified.
     (e) Insulin produced by biotechnology is identical to human insulin and so does not cause allergic reactions as pig insulin can. Insulin is produced much more quickly and cheaply using biotechnology than by isolating pig insulin.